GW01066408

بسم الله الرحمن الرحيم

Muslim Baby Names

English - Urdu with Roman

مُسلمان بچّوں کے نام

رومن ___ اُردو ___ انگریزی

بسم الله الرحمن الرحيم

Published by :
STAR PUBLICATIONS (P) LTD.
NEW DELHI-110002

بسم الله الرحمن الرحيم

English - Urdu with Roman

Muslim Baby Names

(Our 2,000 meaningful and beautiful
names for boys and girls)

Compiled by :

ANJUM NISHĀT

مُسلمان بچّوں کے نام

لڑکوں اور لڑکیوں کیلئے

تقریباً ۲۰۰۰ خوبصورت اور بامعنی ناموں کا انتخاب

مُرتبہ :۔

انجم نِشاط

© Star Publications
ISBN 81-86264-54-3

Published by
STAR PUBLICATIONS (P) LTD.
4/5, Asaf Ali Road,
New Delhi-110002

Reprint : 2008

Price (in India) : Rs. 100/-
(Abroad) : £ 5.95

Printed : Star Print - o - Bind

بسم الله الرحمن الرحيم

WITH HEARTIEST BLESSINGS TO
those boys and girls
WHO WILL BE THE GUARDIANS OF
THEIR COMMUNITY TOMORROW!

بسم الله الرحمن الرحيم

FROM THE PUBLISHERS

All the Muslim names in this book have been included in both Roman (English) and Urdu (Persian) scripts, with meanings of each name in English. The book has been compiled in order of English Alphabets; and for the convenience of readers, we are giving below equivalent Urdu alphabets to English ones :

A	ا ۔ آ ۔ ع		**N**	ن
B	ب ۔ بھ		**O**	او ۔ عو
C	چ		**P**	پ ۔ پھ
D	د ڈ		**Q**	ق
E	ا		**R**	ر ۔ ڑ
F	ف ۔ پھ		**S**	س ش
G	گ ۔ غ		**T**	ت ۔ ٹ
H	ہ ۔ ح		**U**	اُ ۔ عُ
I	اِ		**V**	و
J	ج ۔ جھ		**W**	و
K	ک ۔ خ		**Y**	ی ۔ ے
L	ل		**Z**	ز ۔ ظ ض
M	م			

To simplify correct pronunciation, we have tried to distinguish Alif (ا) and Aa (آ) by putting '~' on the top of 'a' when pronunciation is 'Aa' آ .

၀ ၀၀ ၀

PREFACE

"On the day of Qayamat you will be called by your names and the names of your father's, therefore keep good names."

(Aboo Dawood)

Rasoolullah Sallallahu-alayhi-Wasallam said, "who ever is named after me with the hope of being blessed, he will be blessed and will be in peace till the day of Qayāmat."

It is child's vested right to be honoured with a good name. When choosing a name for the child, it should be done with the intention that the child will be blessed with the 'Barkat' of the name.

It was Rasoolullah's practice to enquire the names of persons and villages while moving to different places. If they were pleasent, it became apparent on his face. If not, his displeasure could be seen.

After birth, the child should be given proper bath. There after the message of the Greatness and Oneness of Allāh Ta'ala and the Prophet-hood of Rasoolullah should be the first words to reach the Child's innocent ears. This should be accomplished by giving 'Azaan' near his right ear and 'Iqaaman' close to his leftear. This noble task should be the prerogative of an 'Ālim' (learned person) or a pious elder of the family. If such a person is not available then any muslim can preform this Sunnat. It is a tradition to remove the child's hair and to observe the 'aqeeqāh', and to name the child on the seventh day after birth. Silver equivalent to the weight of the removed hair, or equivalent value in money, may be given as charity to the poor. 'Aqeeqāh' is a form of 'Sadqāh' whereby the child is safe guarded against misfortunes. Two sheeps or two goats are offered for a boy while one goat or a sheep for a girl, the child being named by a member of the family or by some 'Ālim' venerated by the family.

It is my least effort to provide useful Muslim names for lay readers, parents and scholors.

May 'Allāh' Ta'ala guide us on the Right path. Āmeen.

5th January, 1996   **ANJUM NISHĀT**

(A) ١ - آ - ع

Ababil	ابابیل	.crowd; band; swallow.
Ăbād	آباد	populated; flourishing; inhabited; happy; prosperous.
Ābadāh	عابدہ	endurance; durability; strength; worshippers
Ābādan	ابادان	populated; flourishing
Ābanus	آبنوس	ebony
Abbār	عبّار	strong
Abbās	عبّاس	frowing one.
Abbāsāh	عبّاسہ	lioness.
Abbāsi	عبّاسی	pertaining to Abbās.
Abbāsiyàh	عبّاسیہ	pertaining to Abbās.
Abdāl	ابدال	Plural of Bādal substitutes, persons by whom God continues the world in existence.
Abdāli	ابدالی	relating .to an Abdal, devotee, king who invaded India between A.D. 1748 and A.D. 1767, Ahmad Shah Abdāli.
Ābdār	آبدار	with water shining; wealthy.
Ābdi	عابدی	abbreviated form of Abdul.

Abd Manāf	عبدمناف	servant of Manaf, ancestor of Prophet Mohammad
Abdul Aziz	عبدالعزيز	servant of the Beloved One.
Abdul Ghani	عبدالغنى	servant of the independent one.
Abdul Hamid	عبدالحميد	servant of the praiseworthy.
Abdul Haqq	عبدالحق	servant of the justice and rights.
Abdul Karim	عبدالكريم	servant of the gracious one.
Abdul Latif	عبداللطيف	slave of the subtle one.
Abdullah	عبد الله	servant of God.
Abdul Majid	عبدالمجيد	servant of the exalted one.
Abdul Mālik	عبدالمالك	slave of the lord.
Abdul Mun'im	عبدالمنعم	servant of the beneficialry
Abdul Muttalib	عبدالمطلّب	slave of one who seeks.
Abdul Qādir	عبدالقادر	slave of the powerful one.
Abdul Rahim	عبدالرحيم	servant of the merciful one.
Abdul Rahmān	عبدالرحمن	servant of the merciful one.
Abdul Rashid	عبدالرشيد	servent of the one who guides rightly.
Abdul Razzāq	عبدالرزاق	servant of the provider.
Ābginàh	آبگينه	glass; crystal

Abaha	ابہـا	more or most beautiful; more splendid
Abhāj	ابہـاج	more of most beautiful
Abahar	ابہر	more brilliant; more magnificent
Abahār	أبہـار	(plural of Bahr) seas; rivers; oceans; noble and great men
Ābid	عابد	eternal
Ābid	عابد	spark of fire
Ābid	عابد	worshipper; devotee; devout.
Ābidāh	عابدہ	worshipper; devotee; devout
Ābidin	عابدین	(plural of Abid) worshippers
Ābinus	آبنوس	ebony
Abiq	عبیق	fragrant; redolent; exhaling fragrance
Abir	عبیر	fragrance; scent.
Ābis	عابث	austere; stern.
Ābiyah	عابیہ	handsome
Abkār	ابکار	first borns; virginal; new; novel
Ablāgh	أبلاغ	more or most perfect; very effectual

11

Ablaj	ابلج	shining; beautiful; fair; serence; bright-faced clear
Abrāh	ابَراه	father of the people
Abrār	ابرار	truthful people; saints.
Abrez	اَبريز	pure gold
Abru	ابْرو	eyebrow.
Ābru	آبْرو	honour; dignity
Ābu	آبُ	water lily; lotus
Abu	ابُو	father; lord; master.
Abu 'Abdullah	ابُوعبدالله	father of 'Abdullah'.
Abu 'Ali	ابُوعلی	father of 'Ali. 34th Khalifah
Abu Ayyub	ابُوايوب	father of Ayyub.
Abu Bakr	ابُوبكر	father of a young camel.
Abu Dāud	ابُوداؤد	father of Daud.
Abu Firās	ابُوفراس	father of a lion.
Abu Ghālib	ابُوغالب	father of Ghalib
Abu Hafs	ابُوحفص	father of a lion-cub (lion)
Abu Hanifah	ابُوحنيفہ	father of a pious woman.
Abu Hishām	ابُوحشام	father of Hisham.
Abu Hurairah	ابُوهريره	father of a kitten.
Abu Ja'far	ابُوجعفر	father of Ja'far.
Abu Jahl	ابُوجہل	father of ignorance.

بسم الله الرحمن الرحيم

Abu Lahab	ابو لهب	father of the flame.
Abul 'Aina	ابو العينه	father of 'Aina'
Abul 'Ala	ابو العلى	father of sublimity, the chief
Abul Bashar	ابو البشر	father of man.
Abu Fateh	ابو الفتح	father of (the) victory.
Abul Fazl	ابو الفضل	father of excellence.
Abul Hasan	ابو الحسن	father of the (the) Hasan.
Abul Mäsäkin	ابو المساكين	father of the poor
Abul Qāsim	ابو القاسم	father of Qasim.
Abul Sa'id	ابو السيد	father of the Sa'id
Abul Wafa	ابو الوفا	father of loyalty.
Abu Mansur	ابو منصور	father of Mansur
Abu Qābus	ابو قابوس	father of someone with a handsome face and fine complexions.
Abu Sa'id	ابو سعيد	father of Sa'id.
Abu Saif	ابو سيف	father of a sword.
Abu Sāriyah	ابو ساريه	fater of a column/master.
Abu Sufyān	ابو سفيان	father of Sufyan.
Abu Tālib	ابو طالب	father of a seeker.
Abu Tammām	ابو تمام	fater of Tammam.
Abu Turāb	ابو طراب	father of earth/soil.

13

بسم الله الرحمن الرحيم

Abu 'Ubaidāh	البوعبیده	father of 'Ubaidah'.
Abu 'Umr	ابو عمر	father of 'Umr'.
Abu Y'āqub	ابوليعقوب	father of Ya'qub.
Abu Yusuf	ابو یوسف	father of Yusuf.
Abu Zaid	ابو زید	father of a surplus.
Adā	ا د ا	paying; fulfilling a duty; manner.
Adā	ا د ا	grace; beauty; elegance; graceful manner
Ādāb	آداب	culture; refinement; good breeding; decorum; decency; propriety; humanity.
Ādam	آدم	white camel; black-spotted white deer; human being.
Adālat	عدالت	justice
Adi	عدی	runners, ready to start.
Adib	ادیب	cultured; refined; educated; wellmannered; learned; writer; author
Adibāh	ادیبه	authoress; writer
Ādil	عادل	just upright, sincere; righteous, judge;
Adil	عدیل	equal; alike; just; impartial
Ādilah	عادله	just; upright; righteous

14

Ādil Shah	عادل شاه	king
Adim	عديم	rare; foolish.
Afāf	عفاف	chastity; purity
Āfāq	آفاق	horizons; world; universe
Afarnā	عبغرنا	devouring lion
Afazā	افزا	helper; lord of plenty.
Afāzil	آفاضل	better; excellent; preferable; learned men
Afghān	افغان	lamentation; alas!
Afif	عفيف	pure; decent; virtuous, honest
Afifāh	عفيفه	pure; modest; decent; virtuous; honest.
Afifuddin	عفيف الدين	virtuous of the religion.
Āfil	عافل	setting of the sun
Afkār	افكار	thoughts; meditations; opinions; cares
Afkhām	افخام	greater; greatest
Afkhār	افخار	finest; braver; more splendid; more magnificent
Aflāq	افلاق	heavens; heavenly bodies
Afrāz	افراز	exalted; elevated; summit; height
Āfrin	آفرين	cheers; praise; blessing.
Āfrinā	آفرينه	creator

15

Afroz	افروز	inflaming; kindling.
Afrozāh	افروزه	wick of a lamp
Afrogh	افروغ	rays of the sun; light of a candle; moonbeams
Afsā	افسا	fascinating.
Afsānāh	افسانه	tale; legend; story
Afsar	افسر	crest; crown; ruler; officer.
Afshān	افشاں	sprikled, drops of water.
Afshānāh	افشانہ	one who sprinkles; one who scatters
Afshār	افشار	he who is prompt in his affairs.
Afshin	افشین	spreading far and wide
Afsin	افسین	charm
Afzāl-uddain	افضال الدین	most excellent of the religion.
Āgha	آغا	master; lord; chief; elder brother;
Āghā Khān	آغا خاں	chief prince. title of the head of the Ismal'ili Shi'ahs.
Āghāz	آغاز	beginning; commencement.
Aghlab	اغلب	superior; stronger; with a thick neck.
Aghtaf	اغطف	easy; luxurious; with heavy eyebrows.

16

Ahd	سهـــد	commands; alliances, promise.
Ahmad	احمـــد	most praiseworthy; more commendable, another name of Prophet Mohamad
Ahmadi	ماحمدی	pertaining to Ahmad
Ahmar	احمر	red; rosy; gold.
Ahmari	احمری	red
Ahqāf	احقاف	sand dunes.
Ahrār	ا حرار	noble; freeborn; genuine; free; independent
Ahsan	احسن	beautiful; excellent; lovelier; better;
Aibak	ایبک	messenger; ambassador; slave.
Aiman	ایمن	fortunate; propitious; right;
Aimān	ایمان	oaths
Aimānullah	ایمان الله	righthand side of God;
Aina	عینه	beautiful eyed woman
Aini	عینی	genuine; original; relating to the eyes
Ainullāh	عین الله	eye of God.
Ainul shams	عین الشمس	eye of the sun.
Aisār	اثار	trace; essence;
Āishāh	عائشه	prosperous; fortunate; happy.

بسم الله الرحمن الرحيم

Ājib	عاجِب	unique; rare; wonderful;
Ājibah	عجيبه	wonderful; worth admiration
Ajmal	اجمل	extremely beautiful; handsome.
Akbar	اكبـــر	very big, great.
Akhgar	اخگر	live ashes; spark.
Akhlāq	اخلاق	morals; politeness; virtues.
Akhtar	اختر	star; omen;
Akhtari	اختری	of a star. diviner;
Akhyār	اخيار	good; most excellent
Ākif	عاكف	diligent; constantly employed in devotion
Akkār	عكار	repeatedly attacking
Akmal	اكمل	most complete; perfect
Akram	اكرم	most gracious; precious.
Akrām	اكرام	kindness; generosity
Āl	آل	red colour; tent;
Ālam	عالم	world; universe; time.
Ālamārā	عالم آرا	adorning the world
Alāmat	علامت	signal; mark; symbol;
Ālamgir	عالمگير	holder of the world; conqueror of the world.
Alauddin	علاؤالدين	superiority of religion.
Alawi	علوی	sublime; celestial; heavenly.

18

Ali	علی	high; elevated; august; excellent.
Alim	علیم	learned; sage.
Ālimâh	عالمه	woman of learning; scholar
Alisa	الیساء	God is salvation.
Āliyāh	عالیه	sublime; eminent
Almā	الما	with dark red lips
Almās	الماس	diamond.
Altāf	الطاف	kindness; grace; gifts; courtesy
Altamash	التمش	chief of the army; vanguard.
Amar	امر	order, command
Amir	امیر	dictator, ruler
Amānat	امانت	trust; reliability; trustowrthyness.
Ambar	عنبر	ambergris, night, saffron
Ambarin	عنبرین	of ambergris
Amid	عمید	support; chief; governor; lieutenant
Amil	عامل	worker; ruler; agent
Āmilah	عاملہ	worker; ruler; agent;
Amin	امین	trustworthy; faithful; honest.
Aminah	امینہ	Trust, worthy, honest

Amiq	عميق	deep; profound; widely extensive.
Amir	امير	wealthy; commander; ruler; prince; uncle of Prophet Muhammad
Āmirāh	عامره	rich; royal; flourishing;
Amjad	امجد	glorious; noble
Ammār	عمّار	punctual; tolerant; dignified;
Ammārāh	عمّاره	tolerant; punctual; obedient.
Anas	انس	man; friend; intimacy.
Anāyat	عنايت	favour; grace; patronage;
Andalib	عندليب	nightingale.
Aniq	انيق	beautiful; excellent; pretty;
Aniqāh	انيقه	beautiful; excellent; pretty;
Anis	انيس	companion; friend; lover.
Anisāh	انيسه	companion; faithful friend.
Anjum	النجم	stars
Anjuman	النجمن	congregation; assembly; society.
Ansār	انصار	helpers; assistants.
Anwar	انور	brightest; most beautiful; most glittering
Anwār	انوار	light; lustre; brilliance
Anwari	انوری	of light; shining.

20

Anzar	انظر	florid; shining.
Anzār	انظار	look; outlook; view.
Āqib	عاقب	successor; one who follows;
Aqil	عقیل	prudent; intelligent; wise;
Āqil	عاقل	wise; intelligent; sensible.
Āqilāh	عقیله	wise; popular; intelligent.
Āra	آرا	adorning; embellishing; ornament
Arāfat	عرافت	mount of recognition.
Arfān	عرفان	intelligent; knowing
Ārif	عارف	learned; knowledgeable.
Ārifāh	عارفه	knowledgeable; learned.
Āriz	عارض	cheek; lower part of the ear; army; fledgling bird
Ariz	ارض	firm; firmly rooted; strong; cold.
Arjmand	ارجمند	noble; worthy; honourable
Armughān	ارمغاں	presnt; offering
Arshad	ارشد	upright; honest; obedient;
Arshi	عرشی	heavenly
Arshāq	ارشق	handsome; well proportioned
Arub	عروب	loving wife
Arubāh	عروبه	Friday

21

Aruf	عروف	intelligent; patient;
Arufāh	عروفه	intelligent; patient;
Asadullāh	اسدالله	lion of God.
Āsafuddaulāh	آصف الدوله	head minister of the kingdom.
Asamāh	اسمه	lion
As'ad	اسعد	very virtuous; pious; fortunate; wellbehaved; happier; luckier
Asar	اثر	mark; sign; impression.
Asbāt	اثبات	trustworthy men; arguments; proofs
Asdāf	اصداف	shells; pearls
Āsafiya	آصفیه	pure; clear; just;
Asfurāh	اصفره	prompt; ready
Asghar	اصغر	smallest; minute; youngest.
Ashfāq	اشفاق	favours; kindness; compassion
Ashahar	الشهر	most celebrated; very famous
Āshahub	آشهوب	brilliant stars
Ashi	عشی	evening; night
Āshna	آثنا	friend, well-known
Ashraf	اشرف	very noble; distinguished; eminent;

22

Āshu	عاشو	heavenly
Āshura	عاشوره	10th day of month of Muharram
Āsif	آصف	storm; tempest
Āsifāh	آصفه	storm; tempest
Āsim	عاصم	protector; chaste; virtuous.
Āsimāh	عاصمه	capital city; one who protects; chaste woman.
Āsiyāh	آسیه	support; pillar; strong building.
Askari	عسکری	soldier.
Aslam	اسلم	very safe; protected; happier.
Āsma	اَسماء	very quick of hearing; agreeable; worthy of being heard
Asmāh	اسمه	brave; bold
Asrār	اسرار	secrets
Assāl	اسآل	sweet as honey; honey gatherer; wolf
Āswāb	اثواب	better; best
Ata	عطار	gift; favour; bounty; donation
Atfal	عطفل	children
Atahar	اطهر	very pious; chaste; clean

23

Ataharunnisa	اطهرالنساء	most pious among women
Atid	عتید	ready; prepared; solemn
Atif	عطیف	compassionate; sympathetic; loving; kind
Atifat	عطیفت	grace; favour; solicitude; kindness; affection.
Ātik	عاتک	noble; excellent; pure; bright.
Atik	عتیک	sultry day.
Atiq	عیتق	ancient; liberated; independant.
Atiqāh	عینقة	beautiful; of an honourable family
Ātir	عاطر	fragrant; benevolent; generous; gracious
Ātirah	عاطره	fragrant
Ātish	آتش	fire
Atiyāh	عطیہ	grant; gift; present.
Atuf	عطوف	favourable; compassionate;
Atufāh	عطوفہ	kind woman
Atyāb	اطیاب	clean; noble; refined; excellent
Auj	اوج	top; dignity; promotion.
Aun	عون	help; friendship; friend; helper.

Auqāf	اوقاف	pious foundations; charity institutions
Aurang	اورنگ	glory; honour; power
Aurangzeb	اورنگزیب	embellisher of the throne.
Ausāf	اوصاف	good qualities; praise; virtues
Awwām	عوام	swimmer; swimming.
Ayāgh	ایاغ	cup; glory; gift;
Āyāni	آیانی	politeness
Ayāz	ایاز	respected and enduring.
Ayman	ایمن	oath; very auspicious; right handside.
Ayur	ایور	Eastern wind
Ayyub	ایوب	one who returns; one who asks forgiveness.
Ayyuq	عیوق	pretty; handsome.
Āzād	آزاد	free, independent.
Āzam	اعظم	greater; more powerful
Azamat	عظمت	greatness; grandeur; majesty;
Āzarin	آزرین	garden; gaily attired mistress; manner; custom
Azfar	اظفر	fragrant; pungent
Azhar	اظهر	luminous; brilliant; fresh;

25

Āzif	عاطف	singer; musician
Azim	عظیم / عظیمه	great; dignified; distinguished.
Azimāh		great; dignified; encompassing.
Azimushshān	عظیم الشان	grand; glorious.
Aziz	عزیز	mighty; powerful; beloved
Azizāh	عزیزه	dear; respected; powerful; precious;
Azizi	عزیزی	greatness
Azmat	عظمت	firm; fixed; determination, greatness
Azra	عذرا	virgin; young; unpierced

(B)   نب ۔ بھ

Bābar	بابر	lion, name of Moghul King
Bābil	بابل	gate of God.
Bābirāh	بابره	bracelet
Bābiyāh	بابیہ	miraculous things
Bādiāh	بادیعہ	astonishing; amazing; original
Bādil	بادل	good; religious;
Badi'uzzamān	بدیع الزماں	wonder of the age.
Badr	بدر	perfect state or condition; illumination

Badr-u-Munir	بدرالمنیر	illuminated moon.
Badruddin	بدرالدین	full moon of religion
Badrunnisa	بدرالنساء	full moon among women
Bahādur	بہادر	brave, bold
Bahādur Shāh	بہادرشاہ	brave king.
Bahār	بہار	spring
Bahārbāno	بہاربانو	lady of spring; lady in bloom
Bahāuddin	بہاؤالدین	ornament of religion.
Bahrāwar	بہراآور	favoured; happy; fortunate
Bahrām	بہرام	victory; conquest.
Bairam	بیرم	festival; celebration;
Bakhshād	بخشاد	may God forgive
Bakhshi	بخشی	fortune giver
Bakht	بخت	fortune, luck
Bakhtāwar	بختاور	fortunate; happy; prosperous;
Bakhtiyār	بختیار	fortunate; lucky
Bakhtur	بختور	fortunate
Bākir	باکر	coming early; early morning
Bakr	بکر	young camel
Balāl	بلال	moisture; freshness
Baliq	بلیق	eloquent; complete; effective;

27

Bāni'	بانی	founder; originator; architect;
Bāniyāh	بانیه	founder; originator; architect;
Bāno	بانو	lady; woman of rank
Bānu	بانو	woman, ray of light
Baqāi	بقائی	endurance
Bāqir	باقر	deeply learned;
Barkāt	برکت	blessings; prosperity; good fortune
Barkat	برکت	blessing; abundance; fertility; prosperity;
Bāri	باری	deity; creator; maker.
Bāriq	بارق	flashing; dazzling; lightning;
Bāriqāh	باریقه	lightning; brilliancy
Basar	بصر	seeing; sight; intelligence
Basārat	بصارت	seeing; perceiving; perception;
Bashārāh	بشاره	joyful, happy vision; happy news
Bashārat	بشارت	joyful, happy news
Bāshiq	باشق	hawk; falcon; martin;
Bashir	بشیر	one who gives good tidings
Bāshir	باشر	propitious; auspicious; prudent

28

Bāsiq	باسق	tall; high; lofty; towering.
Bāsir	باصر	one who looks at;
Bāsirāh	باصره	vision, seeing, eye
Basit	بسیط	expanded; spread; ample;
Bāzagha	بازغہ	breaking forth; coming out;
Bātik	باتق	sharp sword
Bātish	باطش	mighty; powerful;
Batutāh	بطوطہ	eathen pitcher; falcon
Bāzigh	بازغ	illuminated; sparking;
Bāzigāh	بازغہ	illuminated; sparkling;
Bāzil	بازیل	generous; liberal;
Bedaār	بیدار	awake; watchful; alert
Beg	بیگ	lord; prince; gentlemen.
Begam	بیگم	lady; woman of rank; wife
Benazir	بے نظیر	incomparable; matchless;
Bilāl	بلال	water; moisture; freshness.
Bilqis	بلقیس	queen of saba, wife of Prophet Suleman
Bismillāh	بسم اللہ	in the name of God.
Bukhāri	بخاری	pertaining to the city of Bukhara in Turkistan.
Burhānuddin	برہان الدین	proof of religion.
Burqān	برقان	shine; glitter;

29

C ‎چ

Chaghtāi	چغتائی	belonging to the tribe of Chaghta.
Chakbast	چکبست	one who measures the ground; one who marks and boundaires.
Chaman	چمن	garden; orchard
Chamanāra	چمن آراء	adorning the garden
Chamanzār	چمن زار	meadow; garden.
Chānd	چاند	moon
Chandan	چندن	sandalwood
Changez	چنگیز	strong; firm; respected;
Chirāgh	چراغ	lamp, light
Chishti	چشتی	belonging to the place called Chisht.

D ‎د - ڈ

Dabir	دبیر	writer; secretary; notary
Dānish	دانش	knowledge; wisdom; intelligence
Dānishara	دانش آره	intelligent, bright (female)
Dānishgar	دانش گر	learned; skilful; wise;
Dāra	دارا	good, nice.

30

Dārāb	داراب	upholder of possessing goodness.
Darafshān	درفشاں	shining; trembling
Dārāh	داره	circle; halo round the moon
Dārāshikoh	داراشکوه	powerful and majestic like Dārā
Darwān	درواں	flake of snow
Daryāb	درياب	knowing, sea
Dastgir	دستگیر	helper; patron; saint.
Dāud	داؤد	beloved; darling; friend.
Diba	ديبا	silk brocade.
Dilāfroz	دل افروز	one who kindles the heart
Dilāra	دل آراء	adorning the heart
Dilāwar	دلاور	brave; bold; heartful
Dilāwez	دل آویز	charming; attractive; fragrant
Dilbahār	دل بہار	heart of the spring season
Dilkusha	دلکشا	heart-expanding; exhilarating
Dilruba	دلربا	heart loving
Dilshād	دلشاد	cheerful; happy
Doshizāh	دوشیزہ	virgin; girl.
Dukhtar	دختر	daughter; girl.
Durafshān	درافشاں	scattering pearls

31

بسم الله الرحمن الرحيم

Durakhshān	درخشاں	brilliance; shining; bright;
Durrāni	درّانی	with pearls.
Durrez	درریز	paral scattering
Durr-e-shahwar	درِشهوار	worthy of a king
Durud	درُود	harvest; mercy; prayer; thanks giving; praise.
Durukhshandāh	درخشنده	shining; resplendent

(F) ف ـ پھ

Fa''āl	فعال	dynamic; great worker
Faghār	فغار	blossom; expand
Fahd	فهد	cheetah
Fahhām	فهّام	very intelligent; learned
Fahim	فہیم	intelligent; quick of understanding
Fahimāh	فہیمہ	intelligent; learned;
Fahl	فہل	with qualities; energetic; brave;
Fahmid	فہمید	understanding; perception
Fahmidāh	فہمیدہ	intelligent; wise; (female)
Fāiq	فائق	superior; surpassing; excellent;
Fāiqāh	فائقہ	surpassing; best; genius; superior

32

Faisal	فيصل	decision; decree; determinatin; judge.
Faiz	فيض	liberal; grace; favour; bounty;
Faizāh	فيضه	liberal; beneficient
Faizān	فيضان	generosity; abundance; benefit
Faizi	فيضي	generous; liberal.
Fakhar	فخر	glory; pride; ornament; grace;
Fākhir	فاخر	proud; precious; honourable; excellent; glorious
Fākhirāh	فاخره	excellent; precious; honourable;
Fakhr	فخر	glory; pride; excelling in glory;
Fakhrat	فخرت	glorious
Fakhruddaulāh	فخرالدوله	pride of the state
Fakhruddin	فخرالدين	pride of religion.
Falāh	فلاح	security; happines; welfare;
Falak	فلك	sky; heaven; firmament; fortune; fate
Falakārāh	فلك آره	one who adorns the sky
Fāni	فاني	perishable; fleeting; changeable; frail.

33

Faqih	فقيه	well versed in religious laws; preceptor; schoolmaster
Farāh	فرح	brisk; playful, joy
Farhat	فرحت	liveliness; ingenuity;
Farāz	فراز	height; elevation;
Farhān	فرحان	glad; joyous; happy
Farhānāh	فرحانه	glad; happy
Farhatullāh	فرحت الله	pleasure of God.
Fari'āh	فاريحه	good natured woman;
Farid	فريد	unique; singular
Faridāh	فريده	unique; pride; large pearl (female)
Fariduddin	فريدالدين	uniqueness of religion
Farih	فرتيح	merry; cheerful; delighted; happy
Farnās	فرناس	thick necked
Farnāz	فرناز	light of pride
Fāruq	فاروق	one who distinguishes between right and wrong.
Farrukh	فروخ	auspicious; blessed; beautiful; happy;
Farzān	فرزان	intelligence; wisdom
Farzānāh	فرزانه	wise; excellent; intelligent; noble; honourable

34

Fasāhat	فصاحت	eloquence; clearness in speech
Fasih	فصیح	eloquent; accurate; plain
Fasil	فصیل	separating; distinguishing;
Fatah	فتح / فاتح	conquest; victory
Fatāhat	فتاحت	help; assistance; conquest; victory
Fātimāh	فاطمه	mother who weans the child, daughter of Profit Mohammad
Fatuh	فتوح	beginning of the spring rains
Fatun	فطون	intelligent; sharp; sagacious
Fauziyāh	فوزیه	victorious; successful
Fayyāz	فیاض	very generous; liberal
Fayyāzāh	فیاضه	very generous; very liberal
Fazal	فضل	excellence; virtue; superiority;
Fāzil	فاضل	scholar; virtuous; proficient.
Fidā	فدا	sacrifice; devotion redemption;
Fidāi	فدائی	one whosacrificedhis life for another
Fazilat	فضیلت	excellence; perfection; virtue

بسم الله الرحمن الرحيم

Firāsat	فراست	intelligence; perception; understanding
Firdaus	فردوس	paradise.
Firdausi	فردوسی	of paradise.
Firoh	فروح	glad; happy
Firoz	فروز	overpowering; victorious; successful;
Firozāh	فروزه	victorious.
Firozbakht	فروزبخت	victorious
Firozbāno	فروز بانو	victorious lady
Firyāl	فریال	decoration; ornamentation
Fughān	فغاں	lamentation; distress;
Furogh	فروغ	splendour; brighness; flame; beauty;
Furoz	فروز	splendour; light; brilliancy;
Furozāh	فروزه	quality; property; description
Furqān	فرقان	distinguishes between falsehood and truth.
Fuzail	فضیل	excellence; virtue; superiority;

(G) گ ۔ غ

Ganjbakhsh	گنج بخش	bestower of treasures.
Ganjur	گنجور	treasurer; rich man

بسم الله الرحمن الرحيم

Gauhar	گوہر	essence; inherent quality, gem, pearl
Gauhardār	گوہردار	bright; glittering
Gauhardil	گوہردل	bold; courageous
Gauhari	گوہری	with inherent qualities; working with jewels
Gauharnisār	گوہرنثار	scattering gems
Gauharpārāh	گوہرپارہ	portion of a gem; as precious as a pearl
Gauharshād	گوہرشاد	cheerful jewel
Gāzid	گازد	gift; present;
Gesu	گیسو	hair; curl; ringlet,
Gesudār	گیسودار	with hair
Gesudarāz	گیسودراز	with long hair
Geti	گیتی	world; universe
Ghād	غاذ	sonftness; tenderness; somoothness
Ghadaq	غدق	spacious; abounding in water
Ghādat	غادت	dawn; morning, young girl
Ghadir	غدیر	stagnant water; pond; pool
Ghaffār	غفار	most forgiving; merciful
Ghaffārāh	غفارہ	most forgivng; merciful
Ghāfir	غافر	forgiving; merciful. another name of God

37

Ghafur	عفور	forgiving; merciful
Ghāli	غالی	one who goes beyond all bounds;
Ghauri	غوری	relating to Ghaur in Afghanistan.
Ghaus	غوث	cry for help; helper; defender;
Ghaus-e-Āzam	غوث اعظم	great helper
Ghawāni	غوانی	beautiful; modest; chaste; singers
Ghayur	غیور	proud in matters of honour or love; zealous;
Ghāzāh	غازه	perfumed powder for the hair and skin; rouge
Ghazāl	غزال	young gazelle, sun.
Ghazal	غزل	lyric, poem;
Ghazālāh	غزاله	fawn; deer; gazelle.
Ghazāli	غزالی	native of Ghazal in Iran.
Ghazanfar	غضنفر	lion, strong
Ghāzi	غازی	brave; who wages war for Islam.
Ghāziuldin	غازی الدین	warrior of religion.
Ghina	غنا	melody; song; air
Ghiyās	غیاث	one who asks for help; one who helps.
Ghiyāsuddin	غیاث الدین	helper of religion.

Ghufrãn	عفران	mercy; forgiveness.
Ghufur	غفور	forgiveness; mercy; pardon
Ghulãm	غلام	slave; servant.
Gulãfroz	گل افروز	dazzling as flower
Gulafshãn	گل فشاں	scattering roses; strewn with flowers
Gulãlãh	گلاله	bunch of flowers; wavy hair;
Gulandãm	گل اندام	with a flower-like body. beautiful; delicate; graceful
Gulbadan	گلبدن	with a flower-like body; with a body like a rose.
Gulbahãr	گل بہار	flower of spring
Gulbãno	گل بانو	lady like a flower
Gulbarg	گلبرگ	rose petal.
Gulbun	گلبن	rose bush; red rose
Gulfãm	گلفام	rosy; with the colour of flowers.
Gulfishãn	گلفشاں	scattering roses;
Guljabin	گل جبیں	with rosy brows;
Gulnãr	گلنار	scarlet
Gulpaikar	گل پیکر	face like a flower
Gulrez	گلریز	shedding flowers; scattering flowers.
Gulrukhsãr	گل رخسار	rosy-cheeked

39

Gulshan	گلشن	garden
Gulzār	گلزار	place where flowers grow.

(H)   ح ۔ ه

Habā	حبا	favourite
Habāqā	حباقا	lotus
Habbāh	حباه	berry, grain or seed; gram;
Habib	حبیب	beloved; sweetheart; darling;
Habibāh	حبیبہ	beloved; sweetheart; darling. another name for the city of Madinah
Habibullāh	حبیب اللہ	beloved of God.
Hadāya	ہدایا	gifts;
Hādi	ہادی	leader; guide.
Hādib	حادب	devoted; benevolent; kind;
Hadid	حدید	iron.
Hadidāh	حدیدہ	piece of iron; iron tool.
Hādiq	حادق	penetrating; clever; sharp
Hadis	حدیث	history; tradition; narration or sayings of Prophet Mohammad
Hādis	حادث	new; fresh;
Haffāf	حفاف	flashing; sparkling;
Hafi	حفی	affectionate; benevolent;

Hafiz/Hāfiz	حفیظ/حافظ	guardian; protector; with a good memory; one who knows the Quran by heart.
Hafizāh	حفیظہ/حافظہ	watcher; guardian; with good memory (female)
Haidar	حیدر	ferocious lion.
Haidari	حیدری	belonging to Haidar.
Hājar	ہاجر	very hot afternoon.
Hājarāh	ہاجرہ	very hot afternoon.
Hājib	حاجب	guard; protector; attendent
Hakim	حکیم	solid; wise; learned.
Hākim	حاکم	chief; lord; ruler; judge; master.
Hāli	حالی	adorned; ornmental.
Hālim	حالم	dreamer
Halim	حلیم	gentle; considerate; mild; gracious;
Halimāh	حلیمہ	gentle; mild; gracious (female)
Hamd	حمد	praise of God.
Hamdam	ہمدم	friend; companion
Hāmid	حامد	one who glorifies; one who praises.
Hamid	حمید	praiseworthy; laudable; glorious.

41

Hamidāh	حميده	one who praises God. (female)
Hamidi	حميدى	pertaining to Hamid; of something praised
Hamim	حميم	7 Surahs of the Quran with letters "Ha" and "Mim", another name of Prophet Mohammad
Hāmin	حامن	protector; defender; guardian;
Hāmir	حامر	clouds which bring plenty of rain
Hammād	حمّاد	one who praises God
Hammādi	حمّادى	pertaining to Hammad; who praises God
Hamra	حمره	red.
Hamud	حمّود	laudable; praiseworthy
Hamzāh	حزه	lion
Hanafi	حنفى	orthodox
Hanān	حنان	love; affection; sympathy;
Hanif	حنيف	one who is inclined.
Hanifāh	حنيظه	one who follows religion, pious
Hannān	حنان	most merciful; most compassionate.
Haq	حق	just; right; true;

42

Harim	حریم	sanctuary; sacred place;
Hāris	حارث	ploughman; planter, lion.
Hārisāh	حارثہ	planter; lioness
Hārun	ہارون	chief; protector; messenger.
Hasan	حسن	pious; beautiful; excellent;
Hasanāt	حسنات	that which cannot be shaken; geantiful, elegant
Hāshim	ہاشم	who breaks bread into broth, modest
Hashmat	حشمت	retinue; great pomp
Hāsib	حاسب	accountant
Hasib	حسیب	esteemed; avenger.
Hasibāh	حسیبہ	reckoner; valued;
Hasin	حسین	beautiful; elegant; handsome
Hasināh	حسینہ	beautiful (female)
Hasrat	حسرت	sigh; regret; anxiety;
Hassan	حسان	pious; wise
Hātim	حاتم	liberal; generous;
Hayā	حیا	decency; modesty; shyness;
Hayāt	حیات	life; existence; animation
Hayātbakhsh	حیات بخش	lifegiving

بسم الله الرحمن الرحيم

Hayi	حیٰ	bashful; chaste
Hāziq	حاذِق	sharp; intelligent; clever; learning the Quran by heart
Hinā	حِنا	Indian hair dye, mehndi
Hisām	حِسام	sword; sword edge
Hishām	حِشام	beneficence; liberty
Hishmat	حِشمت	state; dignity; wealth;
Hudus	حُدوث	novelty; invention; freshness;
Humā	ہُما	bird of good omen; phoenix
Humaid	حُمید	one who glorifies or praises God;
Humaira	حُمیرہ	with a rosy complexion; fair.
Humāyun	ہُمایوں	pertaining to the good omen bird. fortunate; auspicious.
Humrāh	حُمرہ	redness; red coloration; rouge
Hussain	حُسین	pious; handsome.
Husām	حُسام	sharp sword; edge of a sword
Hussān	حُسّان	very beautiful
Husānāh	حُسانہ	very beautiful (female)
Husnā	حُسنہ	beautiful; excellent;

44

(1) ا

Ibād	عباد	servants; slaves;
Ibādullāh	عباءالله	servants of God
Ibn-e-Abbās	ابن عبّاس	son of Abbas, cousin of Prophet Mohammad
Ibn-e-Amir	ابن امیر	son of the King.
Ibn-e-Battutāh	ابن بطوط	son of Battutah, an Arab traveller and author,
Ibrāhim	ابراہیم	father of the people, name of a Prohpet of Islam.
Idris	إدریس	one who instructs
Iffat	عفت	purity; virtue; chastity
Iftikhār	افتخار	pride; honour; grace;
Ifzāl	افضال	eminent; superior;
Ihsān	احسان	benevolent action; favour; charity
Ihtirāf	احتراف	skiful, brilliant
Ihtishām	احتشام	magnificence; glory
I'jāz	اعجاز	miracle; wonder
Ikrām	اکرام	honour; tribute; kindness;
Ilāhi	الہی	divine.
Iltumish	التمش	world conqueror.
Ilyās	الیاس	high as God, great

Imādudaulāh	عمادالدوله	pillar of the Kingdom
Imrān	عمران	prosperity; populaton;
Imroz	امروز	today
Imrul Qais	امرالقیس	man of the Qais, an Arab sacred place
Imtiyāz	امتیاز	distinction
Inām	انعام	gift; reward
Ināyat	عنایت	kindness; grace; favour;
Inshā	انشاء	creation; invention.
Insha'allāh	انشاءالله	God willing.
Inshāt	انشاط	brisk; cheerful
Intakhāb	انتخاب	to choose;
Intizār	انتظار	waiting; anticipation; expectation
Iqbāl	اقبال	advance; approach; response; prosperity;
Iqmār	اقمار	strolling in the moon light.
Iqrār	اقرار	acknowledgment; promise; agreement
Iqtidā	افتدار	imitation; emulation
Irfān	عرفان	recognition; knowledge;
Irshād	ارشاد	command; order; instruction;
Irtizā	ارتضی	approval, acceptance

46

Isbāh	راصباح	dawn, early hours of morning
Isbāt	اِثبات	proof; demonstration; reason;
Isāhāq	اِسحاق	laugher; one who laughs.
Isahār	اِسحار	early sunrise; early in the morning
Ishrat	عشرت	pleasure; mirth; delight
Ishtiyāq	اِشتیاق	fondness; desire;
Islām	اِسلام	Submission to the will of God, Religion of Moslems
Isma'il	اسمعیل	one who has been heard by God.
Ismat	عصمت	honour; chastity; purity; protection
Isrāfil	اسرافیل	one who burns (sacrifices) for God.
Isrā'il	اسرائیل	sincere friend of God; elected. another name for Prophet Ya'qub; country named Israel
Isrār	اِسرار	to hide, mystery
Istiqlāl	اِستقلال	absolute dominion; authority
I'timāduddaulāh	اعتمادالدولہ	confidence of the state
Izhār	اظهار	expression explanation;
Izzat	عزت	dignity; honour; respect;

47

J

ج - جھ

Jabbār	حبّار	almighty; absolute.
Ja'far	جعفر	river; water melon
Jahān	جہان	world; age
Jahānafroz	جہان افروز	enlightening the world.
Jahāngir	جہانگیر	holder of the world.
Jahānpanāh	جہاں پناہ	protector of the world
Jāhid	جاہد	hardworking, industrious; active.
Jāhiz	جاحز	with prominent eyes; with beautiful eyeballs
Jalāl	جلال	grandeur; splendour; glory; majesty.
Jalāluddaulāh	جلال الدولہ	splendour of the kingdom.
Jalāluddin	جلال الدین	splendour of the religion.
Jalib	جلیب	attractive;
Jalil	جلیل	majestic; important; significant;
Jalili	جلیلی	pertaining to greatness
Jalis	جلیس	companion; comrade
Jalisāh	جلیسہ	companion; comrade
Jamāl	جمال	beauty; elegance; good conduct;
Jamāli	جمالی	pertaining to beauty

48

Jamāluddin	جمال الدين	beauty of the religion
Jamil	جميل	beautiful; elegant; good; fair;
Jamilāh	جميله	beautiful; elegant; fair
Jamshed	جمشید	brilliant
Jānafroz	جانفروز	one who kindles life
Jānafza	جان افرا	refreshing of the spirit
Jānān	جانا ں	lover; handsome;
Jāni	جا نی	beloved; friend;
Jān-i-ālam	جان عالم	life of the world
Jarir	جریر	rein, strap; headstall for a camel.
Jāriyāh	جاریه	girl; young woman;
Jāsiyāh	جاثیه	kneeling
Jauhar	جوهر	jewel; gem.
Jawād	جوّاد	bountiful; liberal; kind.
Jawāhir	جواهر	Jewels; gems.
Jāwed	جاوید	lasting; eternal;
Jawwāl	جوّال	wandering; migrant; traveller;
Jāzi	جا ذی	sufficient; equivalent
Jibril	جبرئیل	strong man of God.
Jigar	جگر	liver, heart
Jilāl	جلال	coverings; veils; jasmines

Jināh	جناح	wing; shoulder; arm;
Josh	جوش	heat; passion, excitement
Jugnu	جگنو	firefly; glowworm
Juhi	جوہی	jasmine
Junaid	جنید	small army
Juni	جونی	beauty
Junnār	جنتار	blossom of a pomegranate

K

ک - خ

Kābir	کابیر	great; glorious
Kabir	کبیر	noble; senior
Kabud	کبود	blue; cerulean
Kabudāh	کبوده	gnat-tree
Kāfil	کافل	manager; administrator;
Kafil	کفیل	responsible; guardian;
Kahkashān	کہکشاں	straw-puller, milky, row of stars
Kahlā	کحلا	with collyrium-black eyes
Kaif	کیف	intoxication; mood; humour; delight;
Kaifi	کیفی	intoxicated; exhilarated
Kāināt	کائنات	world; universe
Kalām	کلام	spoken word; speech
Kalāmullāh	کلام اللہ	word of God

Kalim	كليم	speaker
Kalimāh	كليمه	speech; word
Kalāmullāh	كليم الله	one who converses with God.
Kamāl	كمال	whole; perfect; sovereign
Kamāluddaulāh	كمال الدوله	perfection of the kingdom
Kamāluddin	كمال الدين	perfection of the religion.
Kāmil	كامل	perfect; total; complete;
Kāmrān	كامران	successful; fortunate; happy;
Kamshān	كمشان	humble; mild;
Kaniz	كنيز	slave girl; virgin; girl
Karāmat	كرامت	unusual happening; miracle
Karim	كريم	gracious; generous.
Karimāh	كريمه	generous; kind (female)
Karimi	كريمى	liberality; beneficence; grace
Karishmāh	كرشمه	blinking of an eye;
Kashf	كشف	uncover; expose, revelation
Kashfi	كشفى	disclosed; revealed;
Kāshif	كاشف	opener; exhibitor

Kaukab	کوکب	star; constellation.
Kausar	کوثر	abundant; plentiful.
Kāzim	کاظم	one who suppresses his anger
Khadijāh	خدیجہ	premature born
Khādim	خادم	attendant; servant
Khādimāh	خادمہ	female servant
Khādir	خادر	hidden; veilded
Khairuddin	خیرالدین	goodness of religion
Khairullāh	خیراللہ	beneficence of God.
Khaiẓ	خیض	thinker; deliberator
Khālid	خالد	permanent; eternal; everlasting;
Khālidāh	خالدہ	permanent; longlived
Khalil	خلیل	sincere friend; beloved
Khalilullāh	خلیل اللہ	friend of God
Khāliq	خالق	creator
Khaliq	خلیق	kind; suitable; well mannered;
Khamil	خمیل	soft; tender;
Khān	خان	ruler; chief; lord; noble
Khānam	خانم	lady; woman of rank; princess
Khāqāni	خاقانی	imperial; royal

Khārizāh	خارضه	handsome girl
Khasib	خصيب	rich; affluent; fertile;
Khatib	خطيب	preacher; orator
Khatibāh	خطيبه	preacher; orator (female)
Khatif	خطيف	swift; agile
Khāwar	خاور	East
Khayyām	نحتام	tentmaker, name of a famous Persian poet
Khez	خيز	leap; bound; rising
Khilji	خلجى	of Khalaj tribe of Turkey
Khizr	خضر	green
Khubān	خوبان	beautiful
Khubru	خوبرو	lovely faced
Khubsurat	خوبصورت	beautiful
Khubtar	خوب تر	better; more beautiful
Khudābakhsh	خدابخش	given by God
Khuluq	خلوق	nature; politeness;
Khumarāt	خمرات	scent; fragrance
Khuml	خمل	true friend; trusted friend
Khurram	خرم	gay; happy; cheerful;
Khurrami	خرمى	cheerfulness; pleasure; delight;
Khurshed	خورشيد	sun; sunshine
Khurtum	خرطوم	elephant's trunk; nose;

Khushā	خوشا	very good; very nice;
Khushbu	خوشبو	fragrance
Khushbudār	خوشبودار	fragrant
Khushru	خوشرو	beautiful, happy
Khushtab'ā	خوش طبع	of cheerful disposition
Khusrau	خسرو	king; prince; monarch
Khwāhish	خواہش	desire
Khwājāh	خواجہ	lord; chief; master;
Khwesh	خویش	own; self; kinsman
Kibrāh	کبرہ	greatness; pride
Kibriya	کبریا	grandeur; magnificence; glory;
Kirām	کرام	noble; great; eminent; generous
Kirāmi	کرامی	most noble; honourable; precious
Kirdān	کردان	necklace
Kirdār	کردار	conduct; behaviour; character
Kishwar	کشور	climate; country;
Kishwarārā	کشورآرا	one who adorns the country or empire
Kisrawi	کسروی	royal
Kisri	کیسری	royal
Koh-i-nur	کوہ نور	mountain of light

Kulsum	مَكلثُوم	with rosy cheeks; plump;
Kurām	كرام	very noble and generous
Kurd	كُرد	flower-bed
Kurdān	كُردان	necklace of precious metal
Kurrām	كرّام	extremely generous; very beneficent

L ل

La'al	لعل	pearls
Labib	لبيب	wise; intellignet; sensible;
Labiq	لبيق	intelligent; clever; active;
Lahn	لهن	tone; sound; melody; singing of a bird
Lāhut	لاهوت	godhead; divinity; deity
Lāhuti	لاهوتى	divine
Laila	ليلى	black, a famous Arab beloved
Lailāh	ليله	night
Lāiq	لائق	worthy; deserving; suitable;
Laiqāh	لئقه	worthy; deserving (female)
Lais	ليث	lion; strong, capable
Lālā	لاله	incomparable; shining; glitter;
Lālāh	لاله	red tulip; lip of any wild flower; passionate lover; slave

Lālāhrukh	لالہ رُخ	rosy cheeked; tulop cheeked
Lālāzār	لالہ زار	garden of roses/tuips
Lāri	لاری	Persian silver coin
Latāfat	لطافت	freshness; fineness; charm; delicacy;
Latif	لطیف	mysterious; delicate; fine;
Latih	لطیح	intelligent; clever
Libāb	لِباب	prudent; intelligent
Liqā	لِقا	face; vision; observing;
Lisān	لِسان	language; tongue; idiom; dialect
Litāf	لِطاف	thin; delicate; friendly; elegant;
Liyāqat	لیاقت	appropriateness; fitness; decency;
Lubnā	لُبنیٰ	a tree yielding milk sweeter than honey;
Lubub	لبوب	purest and best; essence; prime;
Luhāb	لہاب	heat of fire; flame; blaze;
Luqmān	لقمان	wise; intelligent
Lutf	لطف	pleasure; grace; courtesy; kindness; enjoyment

(M) م

Ma'arif	معارف	face; features
Ma'az	معاز	place of shelter; place of refuge.
Mabsut	مبسوط	extended; large; glad; happy;
Ma'budāh	معبوده	worshipped; adored
Madār	مدار	centre; boundary; goal; orbit;
Maddāh	مداح	praiser, appreciator
Madah	مدح	praise; appreciation
Mafruz	مفروض	necessary to be observed,, ordained by God
Maftun	مفتون	fascinated; captivated;
Maftur	مفطور	created; inborn; natural
Maghfur	مغفور	pardoned; forgiven
Mahāb	مهاب	formidable
Mahab	محب	love; affection; frendship;
Mohabbat	محبت	love; affection friendship;
Mahāmid	محامد	virtues; laudable deeds
Mahbubāh	محبوبه	sweetheart; mistress; beloved

Mahfilāfroz	محفل افروز	one who illuminates an assembly
Mahfilārā	محفل آرا ه	one who adorns an assembly
Mahfuz	محفوظ	preserved; guarded; secure;
Mahjabin	مہ جبین	with a forehead as (face) beautiful as the moon
Mahjub	محجوب	veiled; covered; modest
Mahjubāh	محجوبه	veiled; covered; modest (female)
Mah-iiqa	مہ لقا	vision of the moon
Mahmud	محمود	praiseworthy; laudable; praised
Mahmudāh	محموده	praised; laudable; (female)
Māhpaikar	ماہ پیکر	with a moon-like face
Māhpārāh	ماہ پاره	portion of the moon
Māhpari	ماہ پری	fairy of the moon
Mahru	مہرو	with a moon like face
Māhrukh	ماہ رُخ	with a moonlike face
Mahrum	محروم	disappointed; unfortunate;
Mahshum	محشوم	modest; steady;
Mahsub	محسوب	obedient
Mahtāb	ماہتاب	splendour of the moon

Mahtābi	حهتابى	of moon-like splendour
Mahzuz	محفوظ	delighted; pleased; glad;
Maimun	ميمون	blessed; fortunate; auspicious;
Maimunāh	ميمونہ	tortunate; auspicious (female)
Majāz	مجاز	illusion; passage; corridor;
Mājid	ماجد	glorious; famous;
Majid	مجید	glorious; noble;
Mājidāh	ماجدہ	glorious; honourable; (female)
Makhdum	مخدوم	one who is waited
Makhdumāh	مخدومہ	lady of the house,
Makhfur	محفور	escorted; protected;
Makin	مکین	strong; firm; respected; powerful;
Malak	ملک	angel; messenger;
Malakāh	ملکہ	intellect
Malih	ملیح	attractive; beautiful;
Malihāh	ملیحہ	salty; attractive; beautiful; (female)
Malik	ملک	lord; master
Malikāh	ملکہ	queen
Malikzādāh	ملک زادہ	son of a master

Māluf	مالّوف	familiar; customary; beloved;
Manāf	مناف	elevated, an Arabian doll
Manāzir	مناظِر	views; scenes;
Manizāh	مینِزه	jewel-like lady
Mannān	متّان	very liberal; very generous;
Manshā	منشا	origin; principle; source; motive; aim
Manshur	منشور	spread out
Mansur	منصُور	helped; protected; victorious.
Manzar	منظر	aspect; sight; spectacle; theatre; scene
Manzum	منظُوم	well arranged; poetical;
Manzur	منظُور	admired; approved of; accepted; agreeable
Maqbul	مقبُول	accepted; chosen; satisfactory; welcome
Maqsud	مقصُود	tried; desired
Marghub	مرغُوب	desired; liked; wanted; excellent;
Māriyah	ماریہ	fair complexioned
Ma'ruf	معرُوف	famous; known; celebrated
Maryam	مریم	sour; bitter

Masarrat	مَسَرَّت	pleasure; joy
Masdar	مصدر	source; origin; spring;
Masahaf	مصحف	bound book; page; leaf
Masahafi	مصحفی	pertaining to the book
Mashdud	مشدود	bound; fastened
Mashahad	مشهد	meeting place;
Mashahud	مشهود	present; proved; witnessed; present;
Mashahudāh	مشهوده	present; witnessed (female)
Mashahur	مشهور	celebrated; well known
Mashkur	مشكور	praised; thankful, liked
Mashrab	مشرب	spring; religion; way of life
Mashraf	مشرف	lofty place; height; eminence
Mashaq	مشق	proficient; well-versed;
Mā'shuq	معشوق	beloved; lover
Masih	مسیح	blessed, surveyor
Masnun	مسنون	bright complexioned
Masrur	مسرور	happy; delighted; cheerful
Mas'ud	مسعود	dutiful; obedient; happy;
Mas'udāh	مسعوده	dutiful; obedient; (female)
Mas'udi	مسعودی	happiness; prosperity
Mā'sum	معصوم	innocent; sinless; infallible

Mā'sumāh	معصومه	innocent; simple (female)
Matin	متین	strong; solid; firm
Matināh	متینه	strong; resolute (female)
Matlub	مطلوب	desired; required
Mauj	موج	wave; billow;
Maulud	مولود	born; generated
Mazāhir	مظاهر	appearances; objects; phenomena
Mazhar	مظهر	place of appearance
Māziz	مازینز	excellent; distinguised
Mifrāh	مفراح	very glad; very joyful;
Miftāh	مفتاح	that which brings victory; that which opens
Mihrāb	محراب	warlike; warrior; battle-field; pillar
Mihrān	محران	honeycomb; honey; cotton seed
Mihrbakhsh	مهربخش	bestower of love and kindness
Mihrbān	مهربان	affectionate; kind; friend;
Mihrbāno	مهربانو	lady of the sun; lady of love
Mihrmāh	مهرماه	month of the sun
Mihrpaikar	مهرپیکر	with face like the sun
Mihr-rukh	مهررخ	with a face like the sun

Mihrunnisa	مہرالنساء	sun among women.
Mimrāh	مِمراح	of cheerful disposition; gay tempered; jovial
Minhāj	مِنہاج	way; road
Minhās	مِنہاس	lion
Minhat	مِنحت	gift; benefit; favour; blessing
Mirza	مرزا	son of a king; prince
Misāq	مِساق	treaty; promise; bargain;
Misbāh	مِصباح	lamp; lantern; drinking glass
Misdāq	مِصداق	which verifies a truth;
Mismāh	مِسماح	liberal; bountiful
Mu'ārif	معارِف	one who praises; one who recognise
Mu'azzam	مُعظّم	honoured; revered; dignified; honourable;
Mubārak	مُبارک	auspicious; blessed; august; sacred;
Mubin	مُبین	one who enlightens; one who manifests;
Mubināh	مُبینہ	manifest; clear;
Mufakhir	مُفخِر	one who feels proud
Mufti	مُفتی	jurist; magistrate; wise

Mughis	مغيث	one who answers prayers; one who responds to a call for help;
Mughisuddin	مغيث الدين	helper of the religion
Mughni	مغنى	enricher; rendering competent, singer
Muhammad	محمد	the praised one, Prophet Mohammad
Muhibbuddin	محيب الدين	friend of the religion
Muhibbullāh	محيب الله	friend of God
Muhakam	محكم	strengthened; strong; firm;
Muhsin	محسن	beneficent; charitable, thankful
Muhasināh	محسنه	beneficent; generous; obliging;
Muhsinul-Mulk	محسن الملك	benefactor of the country
Muhtasham	محتشم	great; powerful; wealthy
Muhtasib	محتسب	one who deals in accounts.
Muhyiuddin	محى الدين	restorer of religion
Mu'id	معيد	restorer
Mu'in	معين	helper; supporter
Mu'inuddin	معين الدين	supporter of religion
Mujāhid	مجاهد	one who struggles
Mujib	مجيب	proper; right; fixing.
Mukarram	مكرم	honoured; revered; noble; illustrious

Mukarramãh	مكرمه	honoured; revered; noble; another name for Makkah; another name for the Quran
Mukhayyar	مخيّر	empowered; authorised
Mukhlis	مخلص	devoted; sincere; loyal; pure
Mukhtãr	مختار	empowered; authorised
Mumtãz	ممتاز	distinguished; exquisite; superior;
Munãdim	منادم	companion; intimate friend
Munãzir	مناظر	cirtic; arguer;
Munazzãh	منزّه	pure; blameless; holy;
Munazzil	منزّل	one who degrades.
Munir	منير	splendid; brilliant; shining;
Munirãh	منيره	brilliant; shining
Munis	مونس	intimate friends; companion;
Munasarim	منصرم	manager; administrator;
Munsif	منصف	judge; arbitrator
Muqaddam	مقدّم	first; superior;
Muqim	مقيم	inhabitant; resident;
Muqin	مقين	one who believes
Muqmir	مقمر	moonlit night
Murãd	مراد	intention; desire; purpose;

Murjãn	مرجان	pearl; coral;
Mursalin	مرسلين	messengers; prophets; apostles
Murshid	مرشد	one who shows the right path, guide
Murtazã	مرتضیٰ	desired; chosen; favoured;
Musã	موسیٰ	companion; easy; good work;
Musãhib	مصاحب	companion; comrade;
Musãlih	مصالح	peacemaker; conciliator
Musawwir	مصور	artist; painter; sculpture
Musahaf	مصحف	bound book; volume; another name for the Holy Quran
Mushãhid	مشاہد	spectator; observer
Mushãhidãh	مشاہدہ	sight; vision; spectacle
Musharraf	مشرف	exalted; honoured; respected
Musharrafãh	مشرفہ	exalted; honoured;
Mushfiq	مشفق	kind; merciful; favour
Mushir	مشیر	advisor; secretary; councillor;
Mushrif	مشرف	eminent; examiner
Mushtãq	مشتاق	desirous; hopeful
Mushtari	مشتری	purchaser; buyer
Muslim	مسلم	one who believes in and professes Islam;

Muslimãh	مُسْلِمه	one who professes Islam, obeys the will of God and Prophet Muhammad
Mustafã	مُصْطَفىٰ	chosen; elected.
Mustaghfir	مُسْتَغْفِر	one who asks pardon; one who repents;
Mustaghni	مُسْتَغْنِى	rich; wealthy; idenpendent;
Mustaqim	مُسْتَقِيم	right; straight; proud; proper; harmonious; honest;
Mutabahir	مُسْتَبْحِر	profound; learned; ocean of learning
Muatabar	مُعْتَبَر	honoured; revered; trustworthy
Mutabarik	مُتَبَرِك	blessed; holy; sacred;
Mutãlib	مُطَالِب	claimer; claimant
Mu'taqid	مُعْتَقِد	confident; believable
Mutawalli	مُتَوَلِّى	person endowed with authority; trustee; treasurer of a mosque
Mutawaqqi	مُتَوَقِّى	expectant; hopeful
Mutrib	مُطْرِب	one who brings happiness; delightful; singer
Mutribãh	مُطْرِبه	female singer
Muttalib	مُطَّلِب	seeker; inquirer

67

Muzaffar	منظفَر	victorious; successful; superior;
Muzaffaruddin	منظفَرالدين	superiority of religion
Muzaffarun	منظفَرون	victorious
Muzayyin	مزيّين	adorner; decorator;
Muzfir	منظفَر	victorious; triumphant
Muzzammil	مزّمَل	wrapped

(N) ن

Nabi	نبى	messenger; prophet
Nābigh	نابغ	outstanding; distinguished; gifted; brilliant; talented; genius
Nābighāh	نابغہ	extraordinary genius; eminent;
Nabih	نبيح	celebrated; illustrious; important
Nabil	نبيـل	handsome; intelligent; skilful; clever
Nābilāh	نابلہ	noble; excellent; intelligent
Nabiullāh	نبى الله	messenger of God
Nadā	ندا	dew; moisture
Nadid	نديد	equal; alike; match; rival
Nadim	نديمَ	companion; confidant; friend

68

Nadīmāh	ندیمه	friend; companion (female)
Nādir	نادر	rare; wonderful
Nādirāh	نادره	rare; precious; (female)
Nādiyāh	نادیه	beginning; happening; occurence
Nafāsat	نفاست	refinement; purity; delicacy
Nafis	نفیس	precious; exquisite; delicate; refined;
Nafisāh	نفیسه	chaste; pure; exquisite; (female)
Naghmāh	نغمه	melody; song; musical sound or note or tone; sweet voice;
Nagholāh	نغوله	curling locks of a beautiful woman
Naghz	نغز	beautiful; excellent; good;
Nagināh	نگینه	what fits or sits well, stone, jewel
Nāhid	ناهید	stainless; immaculate
Nāhidāh	ناهیده	stainless; immaculate
Na'im	نعیم	delight; pleasure; benefits;
Na'imāh	نعیمه	delight; pleasure; benefits; ease;
Nairang	نیرنگ	fascination; magic; miracle

Najib	نجيب	excellent; nobe; generous;
Najibāh	نجيبه	excellent; noble; generous; praiseworthy
Najibudaulāh	نجيب الدوله	nobleman of the state
Nājid	ناجد	brave; bold; strong; courageou
Nājidāh	ناجده	brave; bold; strong; courageous
Najm	نجم	star
Najmàh	نجمه	star (female)
Najmi	نجمى	starlike; astral
Najmuddin	نجم الدن	star of religion
Najmunnisa	نجم النساء	star among women
Najmul Sahar	نجم السحر	morning star
Naqa	نقا	purity cleanliness;
Naqi	نقى	clean; pure; excellent
Naqib	نقيب	herald; chief; leader; intelligent person;
Naqibāh	نقيبه	soul; character;
Nāqil	ناقل	reporter; narrator; transcriber
Naqimāh	نقيمه	nature; natural character
Naqiyāh	نقيه	clean; pure
Naqqāsh	نقاش	painter; engraver; sculptor; artist

Naqsh	نقش	painting; embroidery;
Nargis	نرگس	flower resembling the eye, narcissus
Nargisi	نرگسی	flower-like
Narjis	نرجس	eye; flower resembling the eye, narcissus;
Nashāt	نشاط	strength; power; eagerness; zeal; joy;
Nāshirah	ناشره	publisher, exposer.
Nashri	نشری	pertaining to something which spreads
Nashtar	نشتر	lancet; fleam
Nasib	نصیب	fortune; destiny
Nasibāh	نصیبه	providence; luck; fate
Nāsih	ناصح	preacher; adviser; sincere friend;
Nāsik	ناسک	pious; devotee; worshipper,
Nāsikh	ناسخ	one who changes events of things.
Nasim	نسیم	gentle breeze;
Nasimāh	نسیمه	zephyr; gentle breeze;
Nasir	نصیر/ناصر	defender; friend; helper; ally
Nasirāh	نصیره	helper; aide; assistant (female)

Nasiruddaulāh	نصيرالدوله	defender of the state.
Nasiruddin	نصيرالدين	supporter of religion
Nasiyāh	ناصيه	orehead; appearance;
Nasr	نصر	help; aid; support;
Nasrin	نسرين	white rose
Nasrullāh	نصرالله	victory of God
Nastar	نستر	white rose.
Nasuh	نصوح	repentance; sincere friendship
Naubahār	نوبهار	dawn of spring; early spring in full bloom
Naukhez	نوخيز	fresh; tender; new
Naunihāl	نونهال	young; shoot
Nauras	نورس	young; fresh; tender;
Nauroz	نوروز	new day
Naushābāh	نوشابه	water of life;
Naushād	نوشاد	happy.
Naved	نويد	reward; justice; promise; good news;
Nawādir	نوادر	rare; precious;
Nawāz	نواز	cherishing; soothing; playing on music
Nawāzish	نوازش	kindness; politeness; favour; patronage; courtesy

Nawwāb	نواب	great man, rich
Nāz	ناز	blandishment; coquetry; pride; airs, playfulness; gracefulness;
Nazāhat	نزاہت	pleasantness; recreation; purity; respectability
Nazākat	نزاکت	delicacy; neatness; elegance; politeness;
Nāzbāno	ناز بانو	graceful lady
Nāzim	ناظم	one who arranges in order
Nāzir	ناظر	having sight; seeing
Nazir	نظیر	example; instance; precedent;
Nāzirah	ناظرہ	one who sees
Nāzish	نازش	pride; arrogance; glory;
Nazm	نظم	poem, arrangement
Nazmi	نظمی	composer; poet
Nāznin	نازنین	delicate woman
Nazr	نذر	gift; offer
Nazrānāh	نذرانہ	tribute; present
Nāzuki	نازکی	delicacy; softness; tenderness
Nekakhtar	نیک اختر	fortunate star
Nekbakht	نیک بخت	lucky; fortunate

Nekbāz	نیک باز	of good action
Nekdil	نیک دل	kindhearted
Nidā	ندا	sound; voice; call to prayer;
Nigār	نگار	painting; picture; portrait;
Nihād	نهاد	nature; essence; amily
Nilofar	نیلوفر	white waterlily
Niamat	نعمت	favour; graciousness; delicacy;
Niamatullāh	نعمت الله	favour of God
Nisa	نساء	woman; female;
Nisār	نثار	throwing; strewing; sacrifice
Nisbat	نسبت	relation; affinity; reference; alliance; connection; betrothal; relationship by marriage; ratio; comparison
Nishāt	نشاط	happy; cheerful lively
Niyāz	نیاز	offering to a saint, face- to-face meeting;
Niyāzi	نیازی	lover; friend; mistress
Niyazullāh	نیاز الله	offering in the name of God
Nizām	نظام	order; arrangement; administration

74

Nizāmi	نظامی	pertaining to an order
Nizāmuddin	نظام الدین	system of religion
Noshināh	نوشینہ	pleasant drink
Nudrat	ندرت	oddness; singularity;
Nuh	نوح	one who wails, name of a prophet
Nu'mān	نعمان	blood
Nur	نور	light
Nurā	نورا	honourable; respectable
Nurafshān	نورافشاں	increasing light; illuminating
Nurāni	نورانی	light; clear; luminous
Nurbakhsh	نوربخش	bestowing light
Nurbāno	نوربانو	lady of light
Nuri	نوری	of light; luminous
Nurjahān	نورجہاں	light of the world.
Nurmahal	نورمحل	light of the palace
Nuruddin	نورالدین	light of religion
Nurullāh	نورالله	light of God
Nurunnisa	نورالنسار	light amongst women
Nusrat	نصرت	victory; help; support
Nuzhat	نزہت	freshness; pleasure; purity

بسم الله الرحمن الرحيم

P

پ - پھ

Paighām	پیغام	(P) message
Paikar	پیکر	face; form; figure
Pailkarāra	پیکم آرا ر	adorning the face
Pāk	پاک	pure; chaste; innocent;
Pākizāh	پاکیزہ	pure; chaste (female)
Pākruh	پاک رو	sacred soul
Pārāh	پارہ	piece; fragment; gift
Paribāno	پری بانو	lady like a fairy
Parichehra	پری چہرہ	with a fairy like face
Paridār	پری دار	holder of angels
Paridukht	پری دخت	daughter of an angel
Pārināh	پارینہ	old; ancient
Paripaikar	پری پیکر	angel-faced; fairy-faced
Parirukh	پری رخ	beautiful faced
Parirukhsār	پری رخسار	fairy-cheeked; angelic
Parizād	پری زاد	fairy-born
Parizādāh	پری زادہ	fair-born, lovely; pretty
Pārsā	پارسا	watchful; holy man; devotee
Pārsāi	پارسائی	chastity; virtue;
Partāb	پرتاب	leap; tumbling; shining
Parvez	پرویز	victor; victorious

76

Parwāz	پرواز	flight; light; glory; radiance,
Parwin	پرودین	pearls
Pāsbān	پاسبان	guard; custodian
Pāshā	پاشا	king; lord
Pashmināh	پشمینہ	woollen cloth
Payām	پیام	message; fame
Pidram	پدرم	good; charming;
Pindār	پیندار	imagination; thought; ego
Piroz	پیروز	victorious; superior; prosperous;
Pirozāh	پیروزہ	victorious; superior; prosperous
Pirzādāh	پیرزادہ	son of a saint
Purgauhar	پرگوہر	abounding in good qualities; full of intellect

(Q) — ق

Qaan	قان	king of kings
Qābus	قابوس	with a handsome face and fine complexion
Qadar	قدر	divine; fate, respect, appreciation
Qaddām	قدّام	leader; prince; king

Qādir	قادِر	powerful; mighty;
Qādirah	قادِره	potent; powerful; skilful (female)
Qādriyāh	قادريہ	predestined
Qāfi	قافی	follower; attendant
Qāhid	قاحد	single; solitary
Qāhir	قاہر	strong; powerful; victorious;
Qāhirāh	قاہرہ	conqueress;
Qāim	قائم	stationary; stable; present
Qāimuzzamān	قائم الزماں	present throughout the age
Qais	قیس	measuring; comparing;
Qaisar	قیصر	king; caesar;
Qalandar	قلندر	freespirited
Qālun	قالون	good; beautiful
Qamar	قمر	moon
Qamaruddin	قمرالدین	moon of religion
Qamarunnisā	قمرالنساء	moon amongst women
Qarār	قرار	comfort; relief; promise
Qāsid	قاصد	messenger; courier;
Qasid	قصید	aspired; desired; aimed; faultless;
Qāsim	قاسم	one who distributes; equitable

Qāsimah	قاسمه	distributer; just; equitable (female)
Qāsimi	قاسمى	one who distributes justice
Qasr	قصر	castle
Qatil	قتیل	cut
Qatin	قطین	inhabitant; resident
Qayyum	قیوم	self subsisting; everlasting; permanent
Qāzi	قاضی	judge; magistrate; judicial;
Qismat	قسمت	division; distribution, destiny
Qizlbāsh	قزلباش	redhead
Qubād	قباد	beloved; respected
Quddus	قدوس	very holy; pure;
Qudsiyāh	قدسیه	pious; blessed; holy;
Qudus	قدوس	pure; holy; innocent;
Quraish	قریش	gathered from all sides; earn; gain
Qurbān	قربان	approaching near, sacrifice, quiver of arrows
Qurratul'ain	قرة العین	soothing to the eye; delight of the eye
Qutbuddin	قطب الدین	star of religion
Quzah	قزح	multicoloured

79

ⓡ R

ر ـ ڑ

Rabāb	رباب	white cloud
Rabāh	رباح	gain; profit
Rabānāh	ربانہ	violin; fiddle
Rabbāni	ربّانی	divine; godly
Rābi'ah	رابعه	fourth in number
Rābi'ah	ربیعہ	luxuriant; abounding in green foliage
Rābigh	رابغ	luxuriant; pleasant
Rābih	رابح	one who brings gain; gainer; profitable
Rafa'at	رفاعت	high; exalted; nobel
Rafāghat	رفاغت	abundance; affluence
Raffāf	رفّاف	radiant; flashig; sparkling;
Rafi	رفیع	high; noble; delicate with a loud voice
Rafi'ah	رفیعہ	high; noble; elevated; eminent
Rafiq	رفیق	companion; friend; gentle; tender
Rafiqqah	رفیقہ	companion; friend; mistress
Rafi'uddin	رفیع الدین	subimity of the religion

Rāghib	راغب	pray; want; wish; desire
Raghib	رغیب	desired esteemed
Rahābat	رحابت	vastness; spaciousness
Rahbān	رہبان	one who guards the way
Rahbar	رہبر	guide; leader;
Rāhi	راہی	at ease; comfortable, traveller
Rāhil	راحل	traveller, lamb
Rahim	رحیم	compassionate; merciful; kind;
Rahimāh	رحیمہ	compassionate; merciful; kind;
Rahiq	رحیق	pure, generous.
Rahmān	رحمان	merciful; compassionate; gracious;
Rahmāni	رحمانی	divine
Rahmat	رحمت	compassion; mercy; kindness;
Rahmatunnisa	رحمت النساء	compassion among women
Raihān	ریحان	pity; compassion; favour;
Raihānāh	ریحانہ	aromatic plan, favour
Rais	رئیس	leader; superior;
Raisāh	رئیسہ	princess; chief; leader; noble;

Rakhshān	رخشاں	dazzling; shining; resplendent
Rakhshindāh	رخشنده	bright; dazzling;
Ramazān	رمضان	which burns away sins; 9th month of the Islamic year
Rāmish	رامش	ease; joy; harmony;
Ramiz	رميز	agile; prudent; reasonable; intelligent;
Ramizāh	رميزه	active; sharp;intelligent
Ramz	رمز	wink; nod; sigh; intimation; symbol;
Rā'na	رعنا	beautiful; delicate; tender;l
Rāni	رانی	queen or princess
Rashid	رشيد	one who guides rightly
Rashidāh	رشيده	righteous; pious; of good character
Rāshidāh	راشده	one who guides rightly; wise
Rāshiq	راشق	(archer; bowman
Rashiq	رشيق	elegant; graceful;skilful;
Rashiqāh	رشيقه	elegant; graceful;
Rauf	رؤوف	very kind; very merciful; very gracious

Raunaq	رونق	lustre; brightness; beauty; elegance;
Raushanāra	روشن آرار	embellishing with splendour
Rāz	راز	secret; mystery; colour
Razā	رضا	pleased; devoted
Razi	رضی	quiet; easy; gentle;
Raziāh	رضیه	agreeable; happy; satisfied; pleasant
Rāzib	رضیب	gentle, continuous rain
Razwān	رضوان	keeper of vineyard
Razzāq	رزاق	provider of the necessities of life.
Reshamān	ریشماں	made of silk
Rif'at	رفعت	dignity; nobility; promotion
Rihān	ریحان	pity; compassion; favour;
Riyāz	ریاض	teaching; rehearsal, practice
Rizwān	رضوان	consent; pleasure; approval;
Roshan	روشن	luminous; bright; illuminated;
Roshanāra	روشن آرار	embellishing with splendour

Ruhafza	روح افزا	refreshing the spirits;
Ruhi	رُوحی	spiritual;
Ruhinā	رُوحینہ	iron; steel
Rukhsānāh	رُخسانہ	illuminated; shining; glittering
Rukhsār	رُخسار	cheek; face; complexion;
Rukhsh	رُخش	ray of light; sun
Ruknuddaulāh	رُکن الدولہ	pillar of the Kingdom
Ruknuddin	رُکن الدین	pillar of the religion
Ruqayyāh	رُقیہ	progress; height
Rushdi	رُشدی	reasonable; correct
Rustam	رُستم	as strong as steel
Ruswa	رُسوا	debased; dishonoured

(S)   س ـ ش

Sa'ādat	سعادت	prosperity; happiness; graciousness
Sabā	صبا	morning breeze; easterly wind;
Sabāh	صباح	morning; dawn; beautiful
Sabāhat	صباحت	handsomeness; gracefulness; beauty
Sabāt	ثبات	stability; permanence; strength;
Sabihāh	صبیحہ	morning; dawn; beautiful;

84

Sābiq	سابق	first former:
Sābir	صابر	patient; enduring
Sābirāh	صابره	patient; enduring
Sābiyāh	صابیه	damsel; girl
Sabzāh	سبزه	greenery
Sabzināh	سبزینه	young and attractive, beloved
Sa'd	سعد	good fortune; luck; success;
Sadā	صدا	voice; sound; echo
Sadaf	صدف	shell; mother of pearl
Saddām	صدام	one who causes difficulties, brave
Sa'di	سعدی	of good fortune
Sādiq	صادق	true; sincere; faithful
Sādiqāh	صادقه	true; sincere; faithful (female)
Sā'diyāh	سعدیه	good natured; decent
Sadruddin	صدرالدین	leader of the religion
Sa'duddin	سعدالدین	good fortune of relgion
Sa'dullāh	سعدالله	fortunate
Safdar	صفدر	one who breaks the enemy's ranks
Sāfi	صافی	pure; blemishless; bright; shining; flashing

Safinãh	سفينة	ship; boat
Safir	سفير	ambassador; envoy; messenger
Safiuddin	صفى الدين	sincere friend of the religion
Saghir	صغير	minor; small; little
Saghirãh	صغيره	minor; small, little (female)
Sahar	سحر	dawn; morning
Sahar	صحر	grey on red ground
Sahba	صهبا	white and red; blonde
Sãhibãh	صاحبه	lady; wife; friend;
Sãhil	ساحل	coast; seashore; riverbank
Sãhilãh	ساحله	humming; buzzing;
Sãhir	ساحر	magician; enchanter
Sãirãh	ساحره	enchantress
Sa'idãh	سعيده	fortunate; auspicious;
Saif	سيف	sword; sword bearer
Saifuddaulah	سيف الدوله	sword of the kingdom
Saifuddin	سيف الدين	sword of the relgion
Saifullãh	سيف الله	sword of the God
Sãim	صائم	one who keeps a fast
Sa'iqãh	صاعقه	thunderbolt; lightning which falls to the ground
Sãjid	ساجد	who bows in prayer

86

Sājidāh	سَاجِدہ	one who bows in prayer (female)
Sajjād	سجَّاد	composer of rhymed prose
Sākib	ساكب	who pours out
Sākin	ساكِن	quiet, peacable, firm
Salāh	صلاح	advice; honour; peace;
Salāhuddin	صلاح الدين	peace of the religion
Salām	سلام	peace; security; salute
Salāmat	سلامت	safe; well; health; salvation
Sāleh	صالح	pious; good; virtuous;
Sālihāh	صالحہ	virtuous; chaste
Sālim	سالم	healthy; complete; perfect
Salim	سليم	protected; mild; healthy; perfect
Salimāh	سليمہ	mild; healthy; protected;
Saliq	سليق	smooth
Sāliqāh	سليقہ	manner; courtesy; good taste
Salma	سلمٰى	south wind, beautiful woman
Salmān	سلمان	peaceful
Samad	صمد	eternal

87

Saman	سمن	price; value, an Arabic flower (Jasmine)
Samannāz	سمن ناز	pride of jasmine flowers
Samanrukh	سمن رخ	jasmine-faced
Samanzār	سمن زار	garden full of jasmines
Samar	ثمر	fruit; result; wealth; son;
Samarāh	ثمره	fruit; result
Samim	صميم	pure; sincere; just
Samimi	صميمى	cordial; pure; sincere
Samināh	ثمينه	valuable; expensive
Samir	سمير	companion; entertainer; time;
Sami'ullāh	سميع الله	one who listens to God
Sanā	ثناء	praise; applause;
Sanam	صنم	idol, beloved
Sanaubar	صنوبر	pine tree;
Sandal	صندل	sandalwood
Sāniyāh	ثانيه	second; minute
Sanjar	سنجر	hawk; prince; king
Sāqi	ساقى	one who offers a drink, maiden
Sāqif	ثاقف	sagacious; penetrating; intelliget;
Sārā	سارا	pure; excellent; sweetsmelling

Sārāh	سارہ	curtain; shawl; veil
Sarāh	صرح	pure; unmixed
Sarfarāz	سرفراز	superior; victor; glorious;
Sarmad	سرمد	eternal; that which has no beginning or end
Sarosh	سروش	intuition; inspiration; divine obedience
Sarshār	سرشار	brimful
Sartāj	سرتاج	chief; leader
Sarwar	سرور	prince; chief; lord
Sarwari	سروری	empire; sovereignty;
Sarwat	ثروت	fortune; riches; leadership
Sarwat	سروت	one cypress
Sattār	ستار	one who veils carefully; one who pardons.
Satwat	سطوت	power; authority; majesty;
Sa'ud	سعود	auspicious; decent
Saughāt	سوغات	present, gift
Sayyāb	صیاب	one whose aim is true
Shabāb	شباب	youth, prime of life;
Shabāhat	شباہت	similarity; resemblance
Sha'bān	شعبان	interval; month of separation

89

Shabānāh	شبانه	of night; nocturnal
Shabbir	شبیر	ood; virtuous, son of Prophet Harun; another name for Imam Husain
Shabbo	شبو	night smell, fragrant flower
Shabih	شبیہ	image; picture
Shabināh	شبینہ	of night; nocturnal
Shabnam	شبنم	dew
Shād	شاد	light; cheerful
Shādāb	شاداب	green; verdant; fresh; saturated
Shafa'at	شفاعت	intercession; recommendation;
Shafānāh	شفانہ	lark
Shafaq	شفق	compassion; tenderness
Shafi	شفیع	intercessor; mediator
Shafiq	شفیق	affectionate; compassionate; sympathetic;
Shafiqāh	شفیقہ	affectionate; compassionate;
Shafi'ullah	شفیع اللہ	mediator of God
Shahāb	شہاب	red colour, spark of fire ·
Shāh'Ālam	شاہ عالم	king of the world

90

Shahanshāh	شهنشاه	king of kings
Shāhbāno	شاه بانو	lady of the king; queen
Shahbāz	شهباز	brave; royal; generous; noble
Shāhid	شاهد	witness; martyr; one from whom nothing is hidden
Shāhidāh	شاهده	witness earth, pious
Shāhin	شاهين	pertaining to a king.
Shāhināh	شاهينه	pertaining to a king
Shāhir	شاهر	celebrated; popular; famous
Shāhjahān	شاهجهاں	king of the world
Shahla	شهلا	with dark grey eyes.
Shāhnawāz	شاه نواز	beloved of the king
Shahnāz	شهناز	glory of a king
Shāhrukh	شاه رخ	with the face of a king; majestic
Shahryār	شهريار	friend of the city
Shahwār	شهوار	princely; invaluable; worthy of a king
Shahzādāh	شهزاده	heir apparent; prince
Shahzādi	شهزادى	princess
Shaida	شيدا	enchanted
Shaikh	شيخ	chief; elder;

91

Shāima	مشائمه	with a black mole
Sha'irāh	شاعره	poetess
Shāistāh	شائستہ	polite; worthy; honourable;
Shakil	شکیل	pretty; handsome
Shakilāh	شکیله	beautiful
Shākir	شاکر	thankful; grateful
Shākirāh	شاکره	grateful; thankful (female)
Shakur	شکور	thankful; grateful
Shamā	شمع	lamp; candle;
Shamāil	شمائل	figure; face; north; character; nature
Shamim	شمیم	fragrance; perfume; scent;
Shamimāh	شمیمہ	fragrance; sweet smell
Shams	شمس	sun
Shamsā	شمسہ	light; ray
Shamshād	شمشاد	tall and upright tree
Shamshir	شمشیر	sabre; blade; sword
Shamsi	شمسی	belonging to the sun; solar;
Shamsiyāh	شمسیہ	solar
Shamsuddin	شمس الدین	sun of religion
Shamsunnisa	شمس النساء	sun among women

Sharāfat	شرافت	nobility; good manners; decency
Sharafuddaulāh	شرف الدولہ	honour of the kingdom
Sharafuddin	شرف الدین	honour of the religion.
Sharar	شرر	sparks
Sharf	شرف	glorious; nobler
Sharif	شریف	noble; eminent; holy;
Shāriq	شارق	shining; glittering
Shaukat	شوکت	dignity; grandeur; pomp; power;
Shāyistāh	شائستہ	wellmannered; polite; worthy; honourable;
Shāz	شاذ	glad; happy, abnormal
Shāzi	شاذی	gladness
Shāziāh	شاذیہ	rare; extraoridinary; miraculous
Sheftāh	شیفتہ	lover; enamoured
Shibā	شیبا	infatuated; lover
Shibli	شبلی	lile a lion's cub;
Shiguftāh	شگفتہ	blooming; flourishing
Shihāb	شہاب	flame; bright star
Shikeb	شکیب	patience
Shikebāh	شکیبہ	patience (female)

93

بسم الله الرحمن الرحيم

Shimāh	شيمه	natural disposition; character; habits
Shimshād	شمشاد	tall and upright tree
Shirāz	شيراز	cheese, famous city in Iran
Shirin	شيرين	sweet; pleasant; extremely rare
Shitāb	شتاب	speed; quickness
Shu'a	شعاع	sunshine; sunbeam; ray
Shuguftāh	شگفته	blooming; flourishing
Shujā	شجاع	brave; bold; courageous
Shuja'uddaulāh	شجاع الدوله	brave (man) of the kingdom
Sibghat	صبغت	dye; colour;
Sibghatullāh	صبغت الله	colour of God
Sibt	سبط	grandson; descendant;
Sibtain	سبطين	grandsons
Siddiq	صديق	very truthful
Sikandar	سكندر	defender of men; helper of men, a famous King
Simāb	سيماب	quicksilver; mercury
Sinā	ثنار	song; melody; rope; courtyard
Sirāj	سراج	lamp; sun
Sirājuddaulāh	سراج الدوله	light of the kingdom

94

Sirājuddin	سراج الدین	light of religion
Subhān	سبحان	glorifying; praising
Sughrā	صغرا	very small
Suhail	سہیل	canopy; tent
Suhrāb	سہراب	glowing feathers; illustrious
Sulaimān	سلیمان	peaceful
Sultān	سلطان	strength; might; emperor; victory;
Sultānāh	سلطانہ	queen; ruler; empress
Suman	سمن	good repute; fame
Sumbal	سنبل	ear of corn
Surayya	ثریا	rich; lustre
Suri	سوری	beautiful red rose;
Surkhāb	سرخاب	glowing feathers

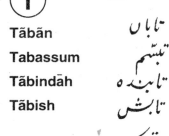

(T)

ت ، ٹ

Tābān	تاباں	light; flash; spark; glitter
Tabassum	تبسم	flowering of a bud, smile
Tābindāh	تابندہ	shining; glittering; bright
Tābish	تابش	splendour; brilliancy; heat; strength
Tabrik	تبریک	good wishes; blessing;
Tabriz	تبریز	challeng

Tafhim	تفہیم	teaching; instructing
Tahabbub	تحبّب	showing love
Tahammul	تحمّل	bearing patiently; patience; endurance; humility
Tahannun	تحنّن	tenderness; affection; sympathy
Tāhir	طاہر	clear; clean; pure;
Tāhirāh	طاہرہ	pure; chaste (female)
Tahmid	تہمید	praising God, religious introductions.
Tahrim	تحریم	to make sacred; to make forbidden
Tahsin	تحسین	praise; chers; beautification;
Tahzib	تہذیب	purifying; adorning; refinement; culture, manners
Tāib	تائب	good; pleasant;
Tāibāh	تائبہ	good; pleasant; sweet; fragrant (female)
Tajammual	تجمّل	adorning; adorned
Tājbakhsh	تاج بخش	bestower of crowns
Tājbāno	تاج بانو	lady of the crown
Tājdār	تاجدار	one who wears a crown
Tajmil	تحمیل	adorning; beautifying

Tajsim	تجسيم	embodiment; relief; magnification; incarnation
Tājuddaulah	تاج الدوله	crown of the kingdom
Tājwar	تاجور	one who wear a crown;
Takbir	تكبير	to praise; to exalt
Takhliq	تخليق	creation; formation
Takmil	تكميل	excellence; completion
Takmilāh	تكميله	perfection; completion (female)
Takrim	تكريم	respect; honour; everence
Tal'at	طلعت	face; appearance; sight
Tālib	طالب	seeker; petitioner; one who desires
Talib	طليب	inquirer; studious; student
Tamaddun	تمدّن	polite manners; refinement;
Tamannā	تمنّا	ambition; desire; culturewish
Tamanni	تمنّى	wish; request; petition
Tamim	تميم	strong; broad; tall; healthy; perfect;
Tamimah	تميمه	charm against witchcraft
Tamkin	تمكين	respect; honour; dignity

97

Tanwir	تنویر	illuminating; shining;
Taqi	تقی	pious; devout; godfearing
Tāra	تارا	star. pupil of the eye
Tarab	طرب	cheerfulness; joy; gladness;
Tarannum	ترنّم	singing; cooing; rhythm
Targhib	ترغیب	stimulating; encouraging inspiring, exciting.
Targhun	ترغون	royal mandate
Tāriq	طارق	anything which appears at night
Tariqāh	طریقہ	path; manner; mode;
Tasadduq	تصدّق	to give alms; to donate
Tasawwur	تصوّر	thought; imagination;
Tasharruf	تشرّف	honour; glory; pride
Tashbib	تشبیب	praising beauty
Tashkir	تشکیر	thanking
Taslim	تسلیم	salutation; obeisance; homage; mercy of God be with you.
Tasnim	تسنیم	anything ·convex and shelving at both sides
Taufiq	توفیق	divine guidance; Go's graciousness; good luck
Tauhid	توحید	considering as one; accepting as one

بسم الله الرحمن الرحيم

Tauqir	تَوقِير	to honour; to respect; to revere
Tausif	تَوصِيف	commending; qualifying
Tausiq	تَوثِيق	strengthening; confirming
Tayyab	طَيِّب	extremely pious and pure, son of Prophet Mohammad
Tayyibāh	طَيِّبه	pious; good; chaste (female)
Taz'in	تَنزِين	to decorate; to adorn
Tufail	طُفَيل	little child; infant

(U)   أ - ع

Ubaid	عُبَيد	small slave
Ubaidāh	عُبَيده	small slave girl
Ubaidullāh	عُبَيد الله	small servant of god
Ubbād	عُبّاد	adorers; worshippers
Ubrud	عُبرُود	tender; relaxed
Ubur	عُبُور	crossing; travelling
Ulfat	ألفت	friendship; attachment, affection
Umair	عُمَير	cultivated and inhabited
Umed	أُمِيد	hope; expectation; dependence; trust;
Ummi	أُمّى	motherly; maternal;

99

Ummul Bani	اُم البنی	mother of sons
Unsur	عنصور	principle; basis; element
Unushāh	عنوشه	fortunate; happy; blessed;
Unwān	عنوان	front; heading
Urfi	عرفی	accumulated; evident; sacred
Urfiyāh	عرفیہ	accumulated; aggrevated;
Usmān	عثمان	young bustard; young animal

W و

Wafā	دفا	faithfulness; loyalty
Wahhāb	ہاب	great bestower; very generous;
Wāhhābāh	وہابہ	giver; bestower; liberal; (female)
Wahhāj	وہاج	very bright; very sparkling; very glowing;
Wāhib	واہب	merciful; generous; donor.
Wāhid	واحد	one
Wahid	وحید	alone; unique; exclusive; matchless; unequalled
Wahidāh	وحیدہ	one; unique; singular (female)

Wajāhāt	وجاهت	respect; appearance; dignity; prestige;
Wajhullāh	وجه الله	presence of God; face of God
Wajahi	وجهی	respectable
Wājid	واجد	finder; inventor; discoverer
Wājidāh	واجده	receiver; discoverer
Wajih	وجيح	thick; strong
Wāli	والی	patron; chief; lord; friend; guardian
Wali	ولی	near; close
Walid	وليد	boy; son; lad; child;
Wālid	والد	father
Walidāh	والده	young girl; daughter;
Wālidāh Sultan	والده سلطان	queen mother
Waliyullāh	ولی الله	guardian of the faith;
Wāmiq	وامق	loving
Waqār	وقار	modesty; mildness; majesty; dignity;
Wāqi	واقی	defender; guardian;
Wāris	وارث	inheritor; heir; successor
Wasi	وصی	executor; guardian nominated
Wāsif	واصف	praiser; describer

101

Wāsil	واصل	arrived; joined; received
Wasim	وسيم	beautiful; handsome; pretty;
Wasimāh	وسيمه	pretty; elegant; beautiful (female)
Wāsiq	واثق	firm; solid; persevering; confident;
Wāsit	واسط	mediator; intervener
Wasiyáh	وصيه	nominated; executor; guardian
Wazir	وزير	one who bears a burden; one who gives refuge; one who strengthens, minister
Wiqār	وقار	modesty; mildness; majesty;

Ⓨ ی ۔ ے

Yāganāh	يگانہ	unique; singular
Yahya	يحیٰی	God's gift
Yaldaram	يلدرم	lightning
Yaman	يمن	right hand or right side
Yambu	ينبُع	spring; fountain;
Yāmin	يامين	oath
Yamin	يمين	right side or right hand
Ya'qub	يعقوب	one who supplants; supplanter

Yāqut	یاقوت	ruby; garnet; gem
Yāsamin	یاسمین	jasmine flower
Yāsir	یاسر	easy; soft; mild;
Yasir	یسیر	small; little; easy
Yusra	یسترا	left side; left hand
Yusuf	یوُسف	handsome as Prophet Yusuf
Yusuf Jamāl	یوُسف جمال	as handsome as Prophet Yusuf

(Z)

زا ـ ظ ـ ط ـ ض

Zafar	نظفر	victory; triumph
Zafaryāb	ظفریاب	victorious; conqueror
Zaharāh	زهرا	shine; sparkle; brilliance;
Zāhid	زاہد	abstinent
Zāhidāh	زاہدہ	abstinent, pious; worshipper; (female)
Zahir	نظهیر	ally; associate; helper
Zahra	زهرا	beautiful; very fair; clear;
Zahur	نظهور	prominent; high
Zaid	زید	necessary; superfluous
Zainab	زینب	ornament, wife of Prophet Mohammad
Zainuddin	زین الدین	ornament of the religion.
Zainul 'Ābidin	زین العابدین	ornament of the believers.

Zaitun	زیتون	olive tree and its fruit
Zakariya	ذکریه	helped by God
Zaki	ذکی	pure; virtuous; just; pious;
Zākir	ذاکر	one who remembers; narrator, another name for God
Zakiyāh	ذکیه	intelligent; clever;
Zamir	ضمیر	in the heart, conscious, thought
Zāmir	ضامر	brave; handsome;
Zarināh	زرینه	golden
Zebā	زیبا	beautiful; graceful;
Zebāra	زیب آرا	beauty; adorning
Zebunnisa	زیب النسا	ornament among women
Zishān	ذیشان	glorious; dignified
Ziyāuddin	ضیاء الدین	light of the religion
Zubaidāh	زبیده	cream; essence; butter
Zubair	زبیر	bright star
Zuhur	ظهور	appearing; visibility; light
Zuhuruddin	ظهورالدین	manifestation of the religion
Zulfaqār	ذوالفقار	owner of spines

=======

جیسے "حمید" کے لئے رومن میں HAMID اور "حامد" کے لئے

رومن میں HĀMID لکھا گیا ہے۔

ہمیں یقین ہے کہ قارئین اس کتاب کو مفید پائیں گے۔

اور نہ صرف اپنے لئے بلکہ اپنے دوست احباب کو بھی یہ کتاب

بطور تحفہ پیش کریں گے تاکہ وہ بھی اپنے بچوں کیلئے خوبصورت

ناموں کا انتخاب کر سکیں۔

انجم نشاط

جمعہ ۵ جنوری ۱۹۹۶ء

تعلق کسی نہ کسی طرح خدا یا کسی اولیاء سے جوڑا جاتا ہے، تاکہ زندگی بھر بچے کو اللہ تعالیٰ کی رحمت اور برکت حاصل ہوتی رہے۔

اسلام میں اس بات پر یقین کیا جاتا ہے کہ ۔ "قیامت کے روز آپ کو آپ کے یا آپ کے والد کے نام سے پکارا جائے گا ۔' اس لئے بھی خوبصورت نام کا انتخاب ضروری ہے۔ آج یوں تو بہت سی ایسی کتابیں موجود ہیں جن سے اسلامی نام کا انتخاب کیا جا سکتا ہے۔ لیکن اس کتاب کی اپنی خصوصیت ہے۔ یہ کتاب انگریزی اور اردو میں یکجا پیش کی جا رہی ہے اور ہر نام کے سامنے انگریزی میں اس نام کے معنی یا اہمیت بھی شامل ہے جو والدین کو بچے کا نام منتخب کرنے میں بہت مددگار ثابت ہوگی۔ اس کے علاوہ ہر نام کو اردو کے ساتھ ساتھ "رومن" میں بھی لکھا گیا ہے تاکہ اردو نہ جاننے والے لوگ بھی اس کا فائدہ اٹھا سکیں۔ رومن میں ان الفاظ کو "جو" ا " کی بجائے "آ" میں بولے جاتے ہیں' کے لئے "A" کے اوپر "زبر" جیسا ایک نشان ڈالا گیا ہے تاکہ نام کا تلفظ ٹھیک ہو سکے ۔

بِسْمِ اللَّهِ الرَّحْمَٰنِ الرَّحِيمِ

پیشِ لفظ

برطانیہ کے ایک نامور مصنف، ولیم شیکسپیئر نے ایک بار
لکھا تھا ۔ ''گلاب تو گلاب ہی کہے گا چاہے اسے کسی بھی نام سے پکارا
جائے'' لیکن مجھے اس سے پورا اتفاق نہیں ہے میرے خیال میں ''گلاب''
لفظ میں اپنی ہی خوبصورتی اور مہک ہے ۔

بچوں کا نام طے کرنے کے معاملے میں بچا ہے وہ کسی بھی قوم یا مذہب سے
تعلق رکھتے ہوں، آج والدین خاص خیال رکھتے ہیں۔ آج سب سے زیادہ
اہمیت اس بات کو دی جاتی ہے کہ بچے کا نام نہ صرف خوبصورت، آسان ہو
بلکہ بامعنیٰ بھی ہو ۔ کیونکہ یہ نام ہی تو بچے کی تا زندگی سب سے بڑی پہچان ہوتی ہے ۔

اسلام آج دنیا کا سب سے بڑا مذہب ہے، مسلمان چاہے دنیا کے کسی بھی
خطے میں رہتے ہوں، اپنے بچے کے نام کو نام خدا ۔ دین ۔ یا تاریخ کے کسی اہم کردار
سے والبتہ کرنا چاہتے ہیں ۔ ان کی زبان چاہے اردو ہو یا عربی یا فارسی، نام کا

بِسْمِ اللهِ الرَّحْمٰنِ الرَّحِيم

اُن بچّوں کی

عُمر درازی کی دعاؤں کے ساتھ

جو کل اپنی قوم کے محافظ ہوں گے!

بسم اللہ الرحمٰن الرحیم

ناشران کی طرف سے

اس کتاب میں مسلم ناموں کو رومن میں بھی لکھا گیا ہے تاکہ جو لوگ اردو پڑھ
نہیں سکتے وہ رومن (انگریزی رسم الخط) سے نام پڑھ سکیں، چونکہ ناموں کو انگریزی
کے تسلسل سے شامل کیا گیا ہے لہٰذا ذیل میں اُن اردو حروف کو انگریزی حروف
کے سامنے درج کیا جا رہا ہے تاکہ قارئین کو کوئی بھی نام یہ لفظ ڈھونڈنے میں
زیادہ مشکل پیش نہ آئے۔

A	ا ۔ آ ۔ ع	N	ن
B	ب ۔ بھ	O	او ۔ عو
C	چ	P	پ ۔ پھ
D	د ۔ ڈ	Q	ق
E	ا	R	ر ۔ ڑ
F	ف ۔ پھ	S	س ۔ ش
G	گ ۔ غ	T	ت ۔ ٹ
H	ہ ۔ ح	U	اُ ۔ ع
I	اِ	V	و
J	ج ۔ جھ	W	و
K	ک ۔ خ	Y	ی ۔ ے
L	ل	Z	ز ۔ ظ ۔ ض
M	م		

English - Urdu with Roman

Muslim Baby Names

(Our 2,000 meaningful and beautiful
names for boys and girls)

Compiled by :

ANJUM NISHĀT

مسلمان بچّوں کے نام

لڑکوں اور لڑکیوں کیلئے

تقریباً ۲۰۰۰ خوبصورت اور بامعنی ناموں کا انتخاب

مُرتبہ :-

انجم نِشاط

بِسْمِ اللهِ الرَّحْمٰنِ الرَّحِيم

ناشران ─────── سٹار پبلیکیشنز (پرائیویٹ) لمیٹڈ
آصف علی روڈ، نئی دہلی ۱۱۰۰۰۲

قیمت (ہندوستان و پاکستان میں) : -Rs. 100/

طابع : لاہوتی فائن آرٹ پریس، سوئی والان، دہلی ۔ ۲